Summary

Online Forex...8

Chapter 1 - Forex: the largest financial market in the world..13

   1.1 - How to enter the Forex.........................17

   1.2 - The main mechanisms that govern the Forex 21

   1.3 - The Pareto principle............................25

   1.4 – What are currencies...........................30

      1.4.1 – Cross majors..................................31

      1.4.2 – Cross Minors 37

      1.4.3 – Exotic currency pairs 39

      1.4.4 – Cryptocurrencies 41

   1.5 – Observe the spread and the pip to get profits..44

   1.6 – Forex trading today 47

- Chapter 2 - How to make money in Forex 52
  - 2.1 – Implementation of a valid strategy 55
    - 2.1.1 – Money Management....................57
    - 2.1.2 – Risk Management 62
  - 2.2 – Trend analysis 68
    - 2.2.1 – Technical Analysis 70
    - 2.2.2. – Fundamental Analysis 78
  - 2.3 – The study of volatility and market expectations...84
  - 2.4 – Signal reception....................................89
- Chapter 3 – Brokers 92
  - 3.1 – Who are the brokers? 93
  - 3.2 – What role do brokers play in Forex?...94
  - 3.3 – How to invest with brokers 96
    - 3.3.1 – CFD 98
    - 3.3.2 – Binary options 99
    - 3.3.3 – Forex 100

- 3.3.4 – Social Trading 101
- 3.3 – Trading platforms 103
- Fundamental Analysis 105
- Chapter 1 - What is Fundamental Analysis 108
  - 1.1 – Main differences between Fundamental Analysis and Technical Analysis 116
  - 1.2 – What is the Fundamental Analysis for? 125
  - 1.3 – Data collection and analysis 134
    - 1.3.1 – Macroeconomic data 139
    - 1.3.2 – Microeconomics data 146
  - 1.4 – Operational difficulties in applying the Fundamental Analysis 150
- Chapter 2 - The financial statements and the Fundamental Analysis 156
  - 2.1 – Budget structure 160
    - 2.1.1 – Balance Sheet 162
    - 2.1.2 – Income Statement 165

2.1.3 – Notes to the financial statements and cash flow statement..........................169

2.2 – Analysis of the financial statement indicators useful for Fundamental Analysis 175

2.2.1 - Earning Before Interest, Taxes, Depreciation and Amortization..............176

2.2.2 – Return On Equity........................179

2.2.3 – Return On Investment................181

Chapter 3 - Fundamental Analysis in the stock market and Forex..183

3.1 – The stock market: sector analysis and company valuation 187

3.2 – The intrinsic value of equities 191

3.2.2 – The market multiples method....198

3.3 – The real estate sector 202

3.4 – Fundamental Analysis in Forex 211

3.4.1 – The Monetary Policy of the Central Banks...217

- 3.4.2 – The economy 218
- 3.4.3 – The trend in gold and oil commodities 220

Conclusions 223

Operating Forex Trading 226

Chapter 1 - What is Forex Trading 230

- 1.1 – How Forex is born 232
- 1.2 – The main advantages 241
- 1.3 – The subjects in the Forex market 247
- 1.4 – Capital management 256
- 1.5 – Forex Trading Indices 264
- 1.6 – The times at which to trade 269
  - 1.6.1 – Forex in America 271
  - 1.6.2 – Forex in Europa 273
  - 1.6.3 – Forex in Asia 275
- 2.1 – Stop-loss 279
- 2.2 – Take Profit 284

- 2.3 – Market orders 289
- 2.4 – Limit orders 292

Chapter 3 - Fundamental Analysis and Technical Analysis 296

- 3.1 – Fundamental Analysis: macroeconomic indicators 302
- 3.2 – The three pillars of Technical Analysis 307
- 3.3 – Dow's Theory 311
- 3.4 – The Momentum and Fibonacci retracements 320
- 3.5 – Overbought and oversold 326
- 4.1 – The moving averages 330
- 4.3 – Relative Strenght Index 334
- 4.4 – Adverage Directional Index 336
- 4.5 – The stochastic oscillator 338

Conclusions 341

7

Online Forex

The Forex market can be imagined from two different points of view. The first image is certainly positive, that is the vision of a financial market that is able to offer anyone the possibility of easily making profits: an opportunity to round up one's salary or even to transform investment into a real work. The second image is negative. The Forex can indeed be seen as a money-eating system, illusory and bankrupt.

In reality, both visions are wrong. In fact, Forex is a system that allows for gains in the medium-long term, but only for those who decide to implement a strategy correctly, dedicating both money and time to the market. In fact, trading is complicated and difficult, but not random activity. This concept is very important as it means that any fluctuation could be anticipated correctly by investors. However, there are a number of theories and tools that can simplify their tasks. But even these tools require time and money to function properly and send the right signals to the trader.

The brokers, with the advent of the internet, have made different platforms available to their users. They have some fundamental indicators and oscillators and translate the oscillatory movements of the market on the charts, so as to simplify their reading.

However, it is necessary to always consider the risks associated with the trading activity. In fact, investments in the financial market offer as many profits as losses. It is impossible to eliminate the negative components, which may be due to incorrect strategies, lateral phases of the market and normal competition present in Forex. The losses, therefore, must be received according to a positive vision, accepting them as much as the profits. It is true that there are few traders who succeed in making profits in the long run, but it is also true that few investors enter the market in a rational manner, without being carried away by revenge or by the will to carry out simple attempts to become rich.

Once the strategy has been implemented, in fact, it is necessary to follow it assiduously, unless it presents some gaps and requires instrumental corrections.

The concept is to "play" responsibly, that is to invest one's capital with the knowledge that success and failure rates can be almost similar. In fact, the first objective must be to develop a strategy capable of minimizing the risks of the trader.

Chapter 1 - Forex: the largest financial market in the world

Forex is considered the largest financial market in the world. This statement is confirmed by the enormous amount of trade volumes that are exchanged daily within it. Forex is also the only market in the world to remain open uninterruptedly for five days a week, allowing traders to make their investments at any time of day or night.

The term Forex is derived from the union of two words, namely Foreign and Exchange, which allow it to be identified as the foreign currency market. Precisely for this reason, it is easy to imagine Forex as the most frenetic market on the entire planet, which at the same time allows traders who decide to invest in it to make greater gains.

To be able to make the trading activity advantageous, however, it is necessary to devote time and money to study Forex and the currencies traded in it, but also to engage in order to implement an investment strategy that allows profits to be made in the medium and long term.

Naturally, as an investment activity, every trader has to study and contemplate the percentage of risk. No strategy, not even that considered almost perfect will be able to guarantee the complete elimination of losses, which however will have to be reduced in such a way as to optimize the relationship between yield and risk. To think of relying totally on chance, on the other hand, is the worst idea an investor who wants to be successful can have.

The fluctuations, albeit minimal and centesimal, relative to the currency trading carried out in the Forex, are not in fact given by chance but are the result of a series of mechanisms and events that the trader must be able to understand. A profit will be made when a trader succeeds in correctly anticipating a future oscillation. Naturally, this profit will increase proportionally to the percentage of risk present in the operation carried out.

It is obvious that each trader will have to implement a strategy based on the objectives he or she aims to achieve. People have different risk appetite and this feature also affects the world of trading.

But there are so many other differences that distinguish one trader from another. For example, in the financial market, investments can be made in a very short time, even within a day, or in a very long time: the choice of the type of trading to opt for will depend on the balance that the trader will be able to give to the relationship between rationality and will to make profits as fast as possible.

1.1 - How to enter the Forex

Getting into Forex today is very simple, but it hasn't always been that way. Until the 1990s, investors who intended to open a specific transaction on the market were forced to physically go to financial agencies or to specific licensed banks. Only after a long wait, due to the countless number of investors, and confusion, could he open his transaction. But even this process did not take place in a timely manner and so opportunities often disappeared and a probable profit soon became a certain loss.

The internet has profoundly changed not only the Forex but also the financial markets. Today, in fact, investing in the Forex market is very simple and it takes just a few moments and a single click to do so. Investments can be made from anywhere: the only requirements are a device with web access and a sufficiently stable internet connection.

Another difference is the costs of entering the market. In fact, every single transaction carried out in the past by an investor was accompanied by very high commission costs. This made trading an exclusive activity for a few subjects, that is, only for those with an initial capital large enough to be able to sustain negative phases of the market that could last for a long time. Today, on the other hand, brokers have decided to cancel commission costs. This decision has an important consequence, as it allows everyone, even those with little or no experience in the world of trading, to access Forex, regardless of thecapital held.

The brokers have therefore attracted an enormous number of subjects, sometimes boasting easy profits, with the aim of increasing market volumes. At the same time, the total opening up of financial markets has given the opportunity even to inexperienced subjects, after periods of study, analysis and experience, to become professional traders.

1.2 - The main mechanisms that govern the Forex

The Forex market is governed by mechanisms that are simple enough to understand, as it is focused on currency trading. This does not mean, however, that trading is easy.

Simplicity lies in the fact that, unlike the stock market and the commodity market, Forex excludes the presence of companies. The value of currencies, that is of the elements of exchange in Forex, is mainly influenced by central banks, which through the implementation of certain monetary policies, influences interest rates and, consequently, the nominal value of money. Therefore, in order to be efficient within Forex, traders will always need to be informed about all the economic and financial events that may affect the Forex market and the items traded in it. As a currency market, it is subject to real fluctuations rather than to trends, which concern stocks and indices.

This difference derives from the fact that, while the indices depend on the willingness of the individual companies to earn, the currencies are tools that represent the economy, and in particular the import and export data of a single nation, and for this reason, they tend more floating in the market. This is to be considered a very favorable characteristic for traders, as it makes Forex much more predictable than all other financial markets.

If the mechanisms of Forex are too complicated to understand and analyze, then it is possible to rely on some tricks that allow you to copy the strategies implemented by professional traders. These techniques, known as Copytrading, can be adapted on the basis of the capital held, allocating only a low percentage of the same for each individual transaction and increasing the investments only if the ratio between yield and risk is sufficiently high.

1.3 - The Pareto principle

The Pareto principle is one of the laws that govern the entire universe. It is a non-physical law, as it has no certain thesis that identifies it, but at the same time, it appears very valid. It is possible to speak of a sort of golden relationship between contrasting elements, in a complete antithesis between them. One of the two elements, in fact, will be numerically or volumetrically larger or wider than the other, in a ratio that is around 80% against 20%.

This principle, as mentioned, regulates the entire universe and, consequently, also the financial markets and specifically the Forex market. Many traders can avoid or disregard this principle, but in reality, it has been statistically stated that about 80% of traders investing in Forex lose the allocated capital. Of course, this data also includes traders who have never studied the basics of trading, nor even analyzed the market. Therefore, going deeper into the mechanisms that govern the Forex would allow traders to move away from 80% Pareto. Nevertheless, it is still statistically confirmed that only 20% of investors manage to pursue a strategy that allows them to constantly make profits.

The Paretian principle applies especially to human psychology and this also applies to the world of trading. The approach to the market and the psychological aspect of the traders are indeed fundamental to understand if the road taken will lead to success or failure. The strategies often fail because the investors do not follow them assiduously, letting themselves be carried away by temptations and not acting on the market with rationality.

The openings of the positions are also regulated by the absolute principle of Pareto. In fact, it is statistically proven that in a well-defined time interval, 80% of it does not allow safe entry into the market, while in the remaining 20%, it is possible to make profitable transactions. Also, in this case, the psychological errors detectable in the haste to open a position or in an attempt to redeem immediately from a negative operation, are to be considered the main elements that lead to failure.

As long as a human remains the architect of his or her own investment, psychological errors will always be protagonists of the financial markets, and the Pareto concept will always have reason to be valid.

1.4 – What are currencies

The currency is considered the object of the Forex market and is considered as the unit of exchange through which it is possible to exchange goods and services. The currency can take both the form of money and be completely virtual. The currency is generally issued by the national central bank.

In Forex, the sale takes place between two different currencies: the currency is the currency of the country. In currency pairs, the first monetary symbol shown represents the base currency, while the second symbol is considered the quote currency. The value of the couple, however, is unique and does not refer to the individual curriculum indicated, but to their relationship. If this value exceeds 1.0, then the first of the two currencies is stronger than the second, vice versa if the value is less than 1.0, then the second currency will be considered the stronger one in the ratio.

1.4.1 – Cross majors

Major or cross major currencies are the most traded currency pairs worldwide, considering the generality of financial markets. They are mainly four and the US dollar is considered as the absolute protagonist, which is, in fact, part of all major pairs.

The main Major is the EUR / USD, or Euro-US Dollar, as these two currencies are the currencies traded in the geographic areas considered to be the most important economies in the world, namely Europe and the United States respectively. Not to be overlooked, this pair also represents the younger cross major, as the European currency has only entered circulation since 2002. Being the main currency pair traded on the market, the EUR / USD shows a very high volatility rate, which translates into reduced spread values. Therefore, traders will find the offers relating to the sale or purchase of these cross majors very easily. The volatility rate is however established both by the ECB, that is, the European Central Bank, and by the FED, or the Federal Reserve, which alter the strength of the controlled currency by increasing or decreasing interest rates.

The USD / JPY, or US Dollar-Japanese Yen, is the second most important Major Pair. Traders take advantage of the difference in value between the two currencies to invest in what is alled carry trading, which is an operation that requires a loan in a country that uses a currency with very low interest rates and then uses the money received to invest in countries with high interest rates. The Japanese Central Bank, or Bank of Japan, has in fact fought low inflation for many years, considerably reducing interest rates, sometimes even wiping them out. Also, for this reason, the JPY is seen as a safe haven, as it shows a positive trend at times when the economy is going through negative phases. Operations of this kind are however complicated and, in order to achieve the set objectives, require a remarkable experience.

Among the cross majors, there was absolutely no lack of the currency pair GBP

/ USD, meaning the British pound-US dollar, known to all traders with the term cable, or the ocean cable used for so many years to communicate the exchange rate between these two currencies. The Pound was the reference currency of all financial markets for many years before the US dollar took its place. The Pound, despite the fact that the United Kingdom has never actually been part of the European Union, links its value and its financial performance to the European economy. Therefore, the volumes included in this cross major can be considered similar to those of the EUR / USD pair. In addition to the Federal

Reserve, the protagonist of this pair is the Bank of England, which modifies the value of its currency on the basis of the monetary policy undertaken.

The last major pair is made up of the US dollar and the Swiss franc, therefore USD / CHF. The Swiss franc is also one the major currencies because it is considered a safe haven. In addition, the stability and perennial neutrality of Switzerland guarantee traders a fairly linear fluctuation in values. Moreover, when the market has relatively low volatility rates, the Swiss franc, due to its geographical position, tends to follow the trend of the Euro.

1.4.2 – Cross Minors

There are a number of currency reports that are not linked to the US dollar, and which are considered to be of lesser importance than the former, and for this reason they are defined as cross-minor. However, these relationships must not be underestimated by traders, either because they influence the major somehow, or because they represent a large part of the Forex volumes. Thus, investors can reap many benefits by investing in the performance of these currency pairs.

The minor crosses relate to the various relationships between the Euro, the Japanese Yen, the British Pound, the Swiss Franc, the Canadian Dollar, the Australian Dollar and the New Zealand Dollar.

To obtain the exchange rates of each minor currency report in the past, it was necessary to convert the base currency into US dollar and then convert it into the quote currency. Today, thanks to the presence of these secondary intersections, the trader is no longer required to carry out this operation and the investments will be faster and more direct.

1.4.3 – Exotic currency pairs

The relationship between one of the four cross major currencies with a currency of economically young or small nations gives birth to an exotic currency pair. Of course, this kind of currencies is traded less frequently on financial markets and within Forex, and for this reason, the commission costs related to individual transactions are generally higher than those related to other currency pairs.

Among the currencies of emerging or smaller countries of note, those of two very important Asian countries stand out, namely Singapore and Hong Kong, but also currencies of countries belonging to the European continent not included in the Eurozone, such as the Turkish Lira and the crowns of the Nordic and Scandinavian countries. Finally, a currency that is becoming increasingly important in the financial market is represented by the South African Rand, which is also included in exotic currency pairs.

1.4.4 – Cryptocurrencies

Cryptocurrencies can be considered as digital currencies without any control by supervisory bodies, and for this reason, it is decentralized. Just the lack of real control has allowed this type of currency to spread easily around the world and to be traded within the financial markets. The main feature of cryptocurrencies is the presence of a very high volatility rate.

The trader will naturally have to foresee the possible evolution of the cryptocurrency observed in the market, trying to buy at relatively low values and then selling at high values. Moreover, even in this market, it is possible to invest by anticipating any future declines in cryptocurrencies, thus selling out in the open.

The best-known cryptocurrency in the world is certainly Bitcoin, which was born in Japan in 2009. Bitcoin was the first cryptocurrency to be accepted as a form of payment on the web. Of course, being totally based on cryptography and on a centralized payment system, known as Proof of Work, Bitcoin has managed to break free from traditional banking circuits, while still guaranteeing the same level of security in digital money exchanges.

To date, cryptocurrencies are therefore used both to buy certain goods or services and to transfer or receive monetary values.

1.5 – Observe the spread and the pip to get profits

Trading in Forex and in all other markets is carried out by considering two essential elements. The first is certainly the price at which a given transaction is sold, and this value is referred to as Bid. The second element is the purchase price of the same operation and it is referred to in a technical jargon as Ask.

The difference between the two elements, namely between Bid and Ask, gives the trader the value of the spread. This difference is nothing more than the commission that each broker receives as gain for every single transaction opened on the market. The calculation of the spread is fundamental for a trader as it helps to identify which transactions are really advantageous, based on the forecasts made and the strategy that the investor has decided to adopt.

Another fundamental element is the percentage of point, also known with the acronym pip. The pip represents the basic unit of the entire Forex, as it indicates the smallest possible fluctuation for a currency pair. Calculating the percentage of point is very simple. It is, in fact, represented by the difference between the fourth decimal digit of the values of a currency pair observed at two different time points.

Since the pip is the unit of measurement of fluctuations within Forex, it is natural that the spread is also expressed in terms of pips. The value of the spread is in any case decided by the broker to whom the trader has decided to rely on. Each investor is therefore required to evaluate the convenience of opening the same transaction with different brokers.

1.6 – Forex trading today

The trading activity has undergone profound changes over the years. The most important of these transformations has certainly occurred with the advent of the web that has practically liberalized the Forex, making it accessible to all.

Today, Forex is considered the safest financial market in the world, as risks are minimized and returns are optimized.

The main advantage of modern online trading is the elimination of commission costs. The brokers, in fact, now make gains only from the spreads calculated on the currency pairs traded in the Forex.

Furthermore, today's Forex allows you to trade at any time of day or night, taking advantage of market openings and closures, depending on their business hours.

Modern trading allows profits to be made despite very low investments. This is possible thanks to the effect of financial leverage, which makes it possible to amplify the investment made even by 300 or 400 times. The higher the possibility of increasing any profit, the greater the risk associated with the transaction. Therefore, it is up to the trader to define and implement his or her own strategy, contemplating all these elements, choosing the most profitable hours and deciding the amount of optimal capital to be allocated for each market segment.

But what most distinguishes modern trading is the fundamental need to understand the market in all its aspects in order to correctly anticipate currency fluctuations. Imagining Forex as a random market is completely wrong. The fluctuations, according to the most important technical analysis theories, are indeed predictable, and there are a number of tools that facilitate the identification of trends and possible future values.

In particular, modern Forex requires the alienation of the emotional component from the investment activity. In fact, humans are excessively exposed to stress and tension, and sometimes open positions on the market driven more by the desire for revenge against a loss just suffered than by rationality. In this sense, we risk sending an entire strategy, even well-designed, into the air with investments that are completely entrusted to chance. This attitude does not characterize successful traders, who follow what they had previously implemented to the letter, accepting losses and waiting patiently for the right time to make the investment.

Chapter 2 - How to make money in Forex

The gain in the world of Forex is a concept linked to both risk and the management of available capital. It is precisely for this reason that it is important to diversify the strategy implemented on several matrices, following different ways to achieve the same goal, namely profit.

Therefore, there is no easy gain even in Forex. In fact, success is the result of a long and tortuous path, which will put traders in difficulty and require time, even a lot of money. So investors will have to find a method of action that minimizes the risk but does not make the yield drop too much. The balance in the relationship between these two factors is to be found in one's own nature. Each person has a different risk appetite than the other, and this is reflected in different strategies in the Forex world.

But trading also requires passion, perseverance, and commitment. Only through these three virtues will a trader engage in the study of fundamental and theoretical concepts, in the analysis of the market and in the implementation of a strategy that can lead to success.

Furthermore, each trader will have to put his or her illusions on one side. In fact, the Forex is a unique world, which offers possibilities that very few other realities are able to grant. However, it is necessary to set goals that are realistic and above all achievable. For inexperienced and novice traders, it is advisable to entrust their investments to a demo account, that is an account that allows the use of fictitious virtual money to carry out Forex trading.

2.1 – Implementation of a valid strategy

So the first real step that every trader must take, after having studied all the mechanisms that regulate the market, is to implement a real strategy that allows him or her to stay in Forex in the long term.

There is no real strategic model that can be considered better than another, but above all, there is no perfect strategy that can completely avoid losses. Of course, there are fundamental concepts that during the implementation phase the trader must try to respect, so as to increase the probability of success. Many experts compare the importance for the trader to create his or her own strategy that adapts to his or her style and goals, to the importance of generating an excellent business plan for companies that intend to establish themselves in the competitive market.

Therefore, the strategy of each trader must focus on two concepts: Money Management, i.e. the management of capital, and Risk Management.

2.1.1 – Money Management

Capital management, known in technical jargon as Money Management, refers to all the operations through which a trader can invest and at the same time protect his or her own capital.

First of all, the trader will have to understand the amount of capital to be allocated for each individual investment. In fact, a strategy consists of more investments, sometimes even contemporary ones, which may be carried out based on different approaches and trading methods. This choice is certainly personal, as it is closely linked to both the investor's risk appetite and the amount of capital he or she has.

Furthermore, a strategy must be implemented in such a way that it can protect the invested capital. Once a trader has opened a certain position, it is necessary to monitor currency fluctuations following a very specific concept: he or she is required to stop losses and let profits run. Therefore, the trader has to identify what are the possible points of exit from the market: letting go of losses in the hope that there is a sudden fluctuation that brings the currency pair back to a position advantageous for him or her is very risky and therefore counterproductive; but letting profits go too far can be harmful, as doing so increases the level of risk more and more, and a sudden price fluctuation could generate a loss. Therefore, the trader must behave in a rational way, and never follow the avarice. Every profit must be seen as a positive operation and never as a missed opportunity.

Even if all these operations, related to the opening and closing of a position within Forex, are delegated by the trader to an automated trading system, the concept just expressed must not be altered. Establishing a correct strategy to define the right time to exit the market is probably more important than achieving excellent entry strategies. In fact, it is precisely in the closure that it is possible to optimize profits or minimize losses.

To be able to monitor all these conditions at the same time, but also to be able to foresee possible future scenarios that could influence, for better or for worse, the open position, the trader can rely on some tools that can generate very useful signals. These signals induce the investor, or the Trading System, to open positions, close them and even reopen them, although the exit from the market has already occurred, in the event that certain conditions are met.

Therefore, Money Management is an element of the strategy that embraces all the phases of trading, from the analysis of the market to the closing of the open positions in it. Many experts consider the management of capital as the fundamental part of the entire currency investment and the causes of possible failure and merits for the possible generation of profits are also attributed it.

2.1.2 – Risk Management

The second element that allows a trader to take the road to success is that relating to risk management, that is, Risk Management. Naturally, the implementation of this process focuses mainly on identifying risky events or strategic components that can generate unwanted risks.

Risk management consists mainly of three modes of action. The first refers to the possibility of transferring risk to third parties, competitors on the market; the second involves the attempt to completely avoid the risk; the third method, finally, involves the acceptance of risk, with the consequent attempt to limit and minimize the negative components.

What the trader must absolutely avoid is the achievement, following a series of losses, of a financial risk, which would entail the total loss of the capital initially allocated in the trading activity.

Once the risks have been identified, the trader is required to analyze them, in order to understand what their actual level of danger is. Therefore, risk assessment allows a strategy to be drawn up which is able to avoid or limit the most urgent risky events, leaving aside those considered less dangerous, at least temporarily. But to get an accurate analysis, the trader should study the actual causes that lead to the generation of the risk and, above all, the consequences that this risk entails. This is certainly the most delicate phase of the entire Risk Management. If you know both the causes and the consequences of a risk, then you can consider yourself able to modify the strategy in an optimal way, in order to minimize the negative results. But this is not always possible within Forex, because of the speed with which the market evolves, and because of the lack of suitable elements to understand the origins and effects of the risk.

Careful evaluation naturally leads to the definition of priorities. The implemented strategy must be able to react promptly to risks, but following both a chronological and economic order. In fact, based on the assessments done on individual risks, the trader will have to decide how much capital to allocate.

This suggests the intense correlation that links Money Management with Risk Management. Both processes are decisive for the implementation of a strategy capable of reacting to internal and external market events, both promptly and with rationality. The task of the trader, therefore, appears very complicated, but even in this case, there are tools that allow to simplify and, above all, to speed up his or her work.

It is therefore very important that every investor, in addition to knowing how to correctly interpret the market, tends to improve in the use of these tools, in such a way as to greatly facilitate its function, delegating to software and automated

systems the tasks that it would have had to perform first person.

2.2 – Trend analysis

Once the trader has analyzed all the internal and external market factors, studied the economic events that could somehow influence the value of the currency pairs and implemented a hypothetically valid strategy, then he or she can move on to analyze the trend or the fluctuations that characterize the Forex.

Many of the analysts of the past have shown that the evolution of the trends is not absolutely accidental, but preventable by examining the historical series, the economic calendar and other social and political events that could influence the financial markets. However, the trend analysis follows two different theoretical directions. The first, based on the assiduous study of the market and trends, is called Technical Analysis; the second, which focuses attention on the events marked on the economic calendar, is called Fundamental Analysis.

2.2.1 – Technical Analysis

The Technical Analysis involves the use of graphs and indicators in order to identify the possible evolution of the currency market. This method of analysis is based on theories of traders and analysts who have over the years succeeded in upsetting the financial market, and making profits in the darkest moments of world economic history.

The main purpose of the Technical Analysis consists of identifying a possible inversion in the trend of a trend. Therefore, the idea is to follow the trend of a trend until it reaches a resistance or support, thus ending up in an overbought or oversold area. At this point, the chances of incurring a turnaround increase and the trader tries to make a profit from the situation that has arisen.

But to understand the actual trend of the trend, the technical analyst must necessarily be based on three fundamental principles. The first states that prices discount everything. This means that, at least theoretically, the trader is not required to study in-depth all the events and factors that can influence a trend, as these conditions are already inherent within the trend. For this reason, it is only necessary to analyze the trend. This is completed with all the information necessary to be able to act correctly on the financial market. The second assumption refers to human behavior. According to the theory of technical analysis, traders tend not to control their emotions, having a euphoric behavior when prices follow a trend and panicking once the trend seems to have exhausted its strength. For this reason, every trend will follow an oscillatory trend, upward and downward, precisely dictated by the behavior of investors. In this sense, it is possible for the technical analyst to identify the possible future evolution of the trend based on his or her past performance. This means that for the Technical Analysis, history repeats itself and it becomes fundamental to analyze the historical series of each trend to obtain advantages in terms of gain by investing in them. The third fundamental assumption of Technical Analysis involves the concept of validity of the trend. In fact, a trend is considered valid until the trader observes clear signs that indicate a reversal. Therefore, a small downward price correction on an uptrend cannot be exchanged for a reversal, which means that the trend has remained valid. This assumption is especially followed by 'trend following,' that is a kind of investors who stubbornly pursue the trend until the actual reversal occurs.

Dow Theory is considered the pinnacle of the entire Technical Analysis. Dow founded his market analysis on six fundamental points, reported in the articles of the Wall Street Journal. The first point of Dow's theory coincides with the first assumption of Technical Analysis, that is, prices discount everything. In the second point of Dow's Theory, a trend is divided according to its gender: primary trend, when it has a duration of more than one year; secondary trend, which can last from three weeks to three months; a minor trend that has a duration of less than three weeks. In the third point, Dow divides the primary trend into three components, depending on the maturation achieved: the accumulation phase, during which the trend is born; the consolidation phase, during which investors identify the new trend and open positions on the market; the third phase, during which the trend loses intensity and the traders close the previously open positions in order to make profits from the price spread. The fourth point of Dow's Theory refers to the fact that if two indices move in the same direction, then the observed trend is still valid. Further confirmation of the validity of the trend must arrive, according to the fifth point of Dow's Theory, from market volumes, which expand or decrease depending on its intensity. Finally, the sixth point indicates the proximity of the trend towards the trader, almost as a sign of friendship. Therefore, the investor must trust the trend until the moment he or she clearly and definitively reverses his or her performance.

The Dow Theory, despite having been written at the beginning of the 20th century, still appears valid and effective. Therefore, the technical analyst is bound to faithfully follow these concepts or to impose them on an automated trading system, in order to succeed in Forex.

In addition to these theoretical concepts, the technical analyst bases his or her investments on certain instruments, such as graphs, indicators and oscillators. Through these, the trader will be able to better understand the market, will perceive the trend of currency pairs and will be able to anticipate future developments.

2.2.2. – Fundamental Analysis

If the technical analyst bases his or her action on the in-depth study of the markets and its historical series, the fundamental analyst focuses more on all those events that can cause fluctuations in trends within Forex. These events can be both budgeted, such as the publication of a balance sheet of an important company active in the financial market of interest, or sudden events, such as the collapse of a political government. The effects of these events can be manifold and the fundamental analyst must be able to understand whether the trends will turn up or down, depending on the currency pair observed.

All relevant economic events must be included in a calendar, which must be regularly consulted by the trader. Future investment strategies will be based on it.

The main element of interest for a fundamental analyst is certainly the financial statements of a company or a major body within Forex. However, to be able to anticipate the trend, the analyst will have to research and study the unofficial balance sheet, generally announced a few days earlier than the actual one. The financial statements, and in particular EBITDA, ROE and ROI must be applied to it in order to understand the state of health of the analyzed company.

The EBITDA is the partial result of the reclassified income statement, which takes into consideration the income deriving solely from the operating management. Therefore, it is the value of income before interest, depreciation, amortization and taxes are added to it algebraically. It indicates the real state of the company, seen not in a particular moment, but in an interval of time. The elements of the Income Statement are flow values, that is in continuous evolution, and not stocks, such as those present in the Balance Sheet. The ROE index, an acronym for Return on Equity, considers the relationship between the net income of the company and its own capital. In this way, the trader is able to understand how much of his or her own financial means used by the company turns into income: the greater this percentage, the better the state of health of the company. Finally, the ROI makes it possible to understand how much of the capital invested has actually turned into income. It is a simple index to apply, but which must be interpreted correctly by the trader to bring about advantages in trading.

The role of the two analysts is in some ways opposite. The technical analyst is obliged to engage in the phase prior to the investment, with an in-depth study of all the historical series, the factors surrounding the Forex environment and with constant monitoring of open positions in the market. Vice versa, the fundamental analyst focuses his or her efforts on the days preceding a specific economic event that can influence the fluctuations of currency pairs, hypothesizing all possible future scenarios based on the economic-financial data of one or more companies and the results obtained by applying the financial statement ratios.

It is impossible to state a priori which of the two methodologies of approach to the market is more advantageous. In fact, each technique has strengths and weaknesses, and each one is better suited to specific market phases. Professional traders carry out several strategies, some based on Technical Analysis and others on Fundamental Analysis, in such a way as to be able to exploit the strengths of both methodologies and cover each other's weaknesses.

2.3 – The study of volatility and market expectations

Volatility is an important indicator of the stability, and consequently of the instability, of a market. It can be calculated on a daily basis or on a periodic basis and allows to know what the actual strength of a trend is, its intensity and, indirectly, its duration. It is possible to consider two different types of volatility, historical and implicit.

Traders use historical volatility to understand what market reactions may be following certain events. They consider the periods characterized by a high or low volatility rate and analyze the responses of the currency pairs to the events marked in the economic calendar. The concept is that the same couple will react similarly to events of a similar nature, and following this idea, it will be more likely to detect future fluctuations in Forex. This type of calculation is best suited to the fundamental analyst.

The implied volatility, on the other hand, is intended to identify the future volatility relating to a specific currency pair. To obtain this indication, the trader is required to compare the curve of demand and supply and all the factors that can influence the trends of these lines. It is a job much more suitable for the technical analyst.

There are numerous tools that can capture and accurately indicate the volatility rate on the market. These tools can be combined together to obtain more precise data and information, optimizing the trader's strategy. In addition to the present and future volatility rate, the charts, indicators and oscillators allow us to obtain important information regarding market expectations. It is possible to find more or less valid information on the web about the future trend of the market, but every investor should research his or her information using his or her own tools, in order to purify the statistics and data obtained from any other influence.

Every active subject has market expectations. If a subject has considerable importance in Forex, then his or her expectation may also influence those of the other subjects. If the general expectation is almost identical, then the trend could really follow that trend, unless there are extraordinary events that alter the market. However, it remains difficult to have a unanimous idea of the market, especially when the strength of buyers and sellers is equivalent.

2.4 – Signal reception

Market expectations can be intuited especially by combining the action of tools and software that allow the market to be analyzed.

Charts are the first tools used by traders. These can be inversion, when they are intended to sense a possible reversal of trend orientation or continuation. The figures that the trends create allow traders to understand what the next evolution of the trend may be, opening and closing positions depending on the time of the market.

The second type of instruments are the oscillators, which draw a hypothetical trend that fluctuates within a range, depending on the values assumed by the market. The oscillators are fundamental to understand if the values of the currency pairs have entered into areas of oversold or overbought so that the trader can invest by acting accordingly.

Finally, the indicators make it possible to follow the market trend. These instruments, unlike oscillators, do not allow to identify areas of inversion, but rather allow the trader to decipher the intensity and strength of the trend, in such a way as to leave his or her position open by exploiting each step. The trend is pursued until it shows an obvious signal of trend variation.

Each tool is very useful for the trader, but to fully exploit its potential, it is necessary to combine their actions. It is only possible in this way to fill some gaps and increase the chances of making profits in the medium-long term.

Chapter 3 – Brokers

In the financial sector and especially in the trading sector, the broker plays a fundamental role, representing the most significant profession in the finance and securities market. The broker market is vast, and each of them offers customers different and personalized services, based on needs. However, brokers do not represent a foolproof system to earn money, as they must always be used without losing sight of the right level of risk beyond which it would be better not to go.

3.1 – Who are the brokers?

Financial brokers are professionals who act as intermediaries between investors and the financial market. In reality, intermediaries that operate in other markets other than financial markets can also be called brokers, such as insurance brokers, shipbrokers, and aeronautical brokers.

The significant figure in the world of trading and investments, however, is that of the financial broker, who today also performs the function of a market maker, that is, deals with the management of the market.

3.2 – What role do brokers play in Forex?

The broker does not only play the role of financial intermediary. In fact, from the legislative point of view, the broker is obliged to protect the investor, informing and covering him or her against risks, but also carrying out assistance duties, both in the phase prior to the investment, and to that strictly inherent to the same.

Over the years, with the transformation of the financial market, the role of the broker has also changed. Initially, the intermediaries made gains especially from the commissions, which until a few decades ago turned out to be very high. Nowadays, the brokers, also covering a task of protecting investors, have reduced or even zeroed the cost related to the commissions for opening transactions in the Forex. Their profits today are generated with spreads, that is with the price difference between two values of the same currency pair observed in two different periods.

So the brokers work alongside the traders during each investment phase, supporting and protecting them, so as to allow them to stay on the market for as long as possible.

3.3 – How to invest with brokers

In order to make investments on the Forex and on any other financial market, it is necessary to understand what the evolution of a trend is and to open a position following the hypotheses carried out. However, the trader must understand the dynamics of growth of the trend, and through a well-implemented technical analysis, study the time series, comparing the possible evolutions and reactions of the trends.

The trader must also clearly define their goals. In fact, if for some people trading represents a moment of leisure, for others it has become a real job. This is why it is best for each investor to categorize himself or herself into a certain class, thus also defining his or her own role in Forex.

3.3.1 – CFD

The acronym CFD means the Contract for Difference: the trader can invest in the difference in value of a particular financial instrument, from the moment in which the position in the market is opened to the moment in which it is closed.

This type of investment has involved an increasing number of people, becoming one of the most popular assets in the world. This is because there is no real purchase of securities, and the problem of exchange rates is also eliminated.

3.3.2 – Binary options

Binary options are short and medium-term investment methods. It is simply a matter of opening a position to a certain value of the observed trend and understanding whether the evolution within a well-defined range is up or down. It is a type of investment appreciated precisely because it allows traders to make profits even within a few minutes.

3.3.3 – Forex

Forex is the financial market par excellence. Each broker allows you to open positions in this market, as there is a guarantee of high values of trading volumes and a complete opening, with the consequent possibility of investment, round the clock. The Forex is an unlimited market, both from a temporal and a financial point of view, as it offers greater guarantees of success than any other market.

3.3.4 – Social Trading

The new frontier of trading offers the possibility of combining investment strategies with social networks. In fact, there are platforms that allow traders to make public the strategies implemented, to ask other users for advice on specific processes inherent in them and to share strengths and weaknesses of their analysis with everyone. More and more professional traders decide to subscribe to these social platforms to hone their skills and provide support to all those who come across Forex for the first time.

This methodology also makes it possible to collectively understand certain market processes that can prove to be excessively complex. It is a highly appreciated methodology, which in recent years is spreading more and more, all over the world.

3.3 – Trading platforms

Each broker provides its users with a platform that acts as an interface between the trader and the financial market. Generally, these platforms have various tools, such as charts, oscillators and indicators, able to send signals to the investor, suggesting the opening and closing of positions.

There are both free platforms that can be downloaded directly from the web and paid platforms. The paid platforms differ from the free ones for greater clarity in the offered analysis, a better interpretation of the evolution of the market and a more correct individualization of the possible evolution of the trend.

The platforms are created especially for those who are entering the financial market for the first time and who need to become familiar with the techniques to be used and the strategies to be implemented.

www.ingramcontent.com/pod-product-compliance
Lightning Source LLC
Chambersburg PA
CBHW070424220526
45466CB00004B/1528